ent !!

Lots of love,

Anita and Chris

xo

The A-Z of Retirement

The A-Z of Retirement

Frank Schroder

Central Queensland
UNIVERSITY
PRESS

First published in 2004 by Central Queensland University Press

Distributed by:
CQU Press
PO Box 1615
Rockhampton Queensland 4700
Ph: (07) 4923 2520
Fax: (07) 4923 2525
Email: cqupress@cqu.edu.au
www.outbackbooks.com

National Library of Australia
Cataloguing-in-Publication data:

Schroder, Frank.
The A-Z of retirement : are you a GOM (Grumpy old man).

ISBN 1 876780 54 1.

1. Retirement.
2. Men - Retirement - Health aspects.
3. Men - Retirement - Psychological aspects.

I. Title.

306.38

Cover design and typesetting by Jane Dorrington
Printed and bound by Watson Ferguson and Co., Brisbane

Front cover image and cartoons by Mike Swain, Noosa.

Acknowledgements

Firstly I would like to thank my wife, Heather, without whose help and encouragement I could never have brought it all together. She helped in so many ways, not only with ideas of what I might include, but also the clearest ways of expressing them. Each and every word is important.

I would particularly like to thank Bob Hay for encouraging me to write a book in the first place. He had more confidence in me than I had. Without his encouragement I would never have begun.

I also wish to thank a number of people who have given me considerable help with encouragement, in proof reading and offering suggestions for this book. These include Mary Wharmby, Evelyn Smith, Colin Smith, Rachael Mecham, Jacquie Tonkin and Fiona Foley.

There are many others, of course, who contributed without knowing it, and I feel indebted to them, also. Ideas come from anywhere and everywhere. If you recognise yourself in the text I'm more than happy.

I would especially like to thank Mick Swain who created the cartoons and those two colour photographs, which I think are particularly appropriate. The RADF, through Noosa Council, has been very helpful in funding this artwork.

Finally, the person who had the biggest contribution in shaping the book, with ideas, criticism and editing, was Professor David Myers, the editor of Central Queensland University - Old Silvertail's Outback Books. He deserves loads of thanks. I cannot overstate the enormous task he undertook to make me take a paradigm shift in my approach to writing about this subject. Thanks a million, David. I'll always be in your debt, and I've learnt such a lot.

However, I take full responsibility for the content of the book and all the errors. I don't expect everybody to agree with all the sentiments in the book. If such were the case the book would be redundant.

Frank Schroder
2004.

Contents

You Blokes in Retirement!
A Message

Follow the simple advice set out in this book and a happy retirement is assured. There is no need to be a GOM (Grumpy Old Man).

No fortune required

No drugs required

No booze required

You will have more:

- Adventure
- Social activity
- Self-esteem and fulfilment
- Feeling of contribution to your community
- Relaxed harmony with your partner

Forget the single-minded pursuit of wealth and enjoy every moment of every day

> Remember: Forty years of work is the worst possible training for an exciting and happy retirement

INFANCY

CHILDHOOD

ADULTHOOD

OBSOLESCENCE

SWAIN

The Typical Male Lifecycle
The Ups and the Downs

The following stages describe the male lifestyle

Stage 1 :: Childhood

Fun and Games. Backyard football, cricket, cowboys & indians, cops & robbers. Lots of laughs and a few bruises.

Stage 2 :: Study Years

Some serious learning. The opposite sex, confusion, adventure & topsy-turvy fun.

Stage 3 :: Work

Making money, getting a wife and family, buying a house and holding down a responsible job. Investing in security and superannuation. More worries than fun.

Stage 4 :: 1st Year Retirement - Initial Excitement

Making the grand trip around Australia or overseas. Looking forward to leisure. Getting the house and garden in first-class order.

Stage 5 :: Long Term Retirement - Big Emotional Problems

Being bored. Being rejected — people have forgotten who you were. Not having enough friends or activities. Eating and drinking too much. Unwanted at home - the wife wants you out of the house. Going down the track to depression and possible divorce.

> Do you remember your youth, when Mother had to call you in from your games for meals, and you didn't want to come because you were having too much fun playing? Retirement can be just as much fun! Recapture your youth.

Test Yourself:
Are You Happy in Retirement?

Test yourself! How do you rate?
Are you a miserable, grumpy, listless, unmotivated, resentful RETIREE?

1. Do you spend more than three hours a day watching TV?   Yes ☐   No ☐

2. Do you lie in bed in the morning because you can't think of any reason to get up?   Yes ☐   No ☐

3. Do you feel resentful that no one remembers how important you were when you were a professional or a big time manager?   Yes ☐   No ☐

4. Are you eating too much and drinking too much because you can't think what to do with yourself?   Yes ☐   No ☐

5. Have you run out of friends?   Yes ☐   No ☐

6. Do your friends irritate you and annoy you?   Yes ☐   No ☐

7. Is your wife desperately trying to get you out of the house?   Yes ☐   No ☐

8. Are you a member of any clubs?   Yes ☐   No ☐

9. Do you play any sports?   Yes ☐   No ☐

10. Do you walk at least two kilometres every day?   Yes ☐   No ☐

11. Are you angry with your ageing body?   Yes ☐   No ☐

12. Do you write letters to the editor of the local newspaper?   Yes ☐   No ☐

13. Are you a member of the U3A?   Yes ☐   No ☐

14. Is it more than two weeks since you visited your local library and borrowed a book?   Yes ☐   No ☐

15. Are you a member of a book discussion group?   Yes ☐   No ☐

16. Are you a member of a film discussion group?   Yes ☐   No ☐

17. Are you a member of any of the Service Clubs?   Yes ☐   No ☐

18. Are you worried about people not remembering who you are (or were)?   Yes ☐   No ☐

19. Do you go out to dinner or to the movies in big groups?   Yes ☐   No ☐

20. Do you get pleasure and joy from your pets, or from your garden?   Yes ☐   No ☐

Scoring

1.   Yes - 10   No - 0
2.   Yes - 10   No - 0
3.   Yes - 10   No - 0
4.   Yes - 10   No - 0
5.   Yes - 10   No - 0
6.   Yes - 10   No - 0
7.   Yes - 10   No - 0
8.   Yes - 0   No - 10
9.   Yes - 0   No - 10
10.   Yes - 0   No - 10
11.   Yes - 10   No - 0
12.   Yes - 0   No - 10
13.   Yes - 0   No - 10
14.   Yes - 10   No - 0
15.   Yes - 0   No - 10
16.   Yes - 0   No - 10
17.   Yes - 0   No - 10
18.   Yes - 0   No - 10
19.   Yes - 0   No - 10
20.   Yes - 0   No - 10

0-40 points

Congratulations!

You're getting the best out of your retirement that you possibly can. No GOM here.

50-70 points

Hmm...

You're not getting as much as you could out of your retirement. Liven it up a little!

80 + points

Argh!

You're in BIG trouble and you need to read this book and CHANGE YOUR LIFE (with your partner's help)!

Is There a Problem...
With Male Retirees?

Yes there is:
Women resent those of us that are GOMs!

Here are some recent trends that cause concern.

- Many retired men are grumpy and depressed, with little to do. They frequently turn into couch potatoes with square eyes. Or they become compulsive gamblers because they have lost all sense of excitement about daily life. Or they get sloshed on booze every day or stuff themselves with food. They are in a crisis and they don't know it.

- Many retired women are envious of their daughter's new found freedom. The daughters are living happier lives without a male partner.

- Many retired men report boredom and a lack of purpose soon after retirement.

- Widows are more likely to be happier (after a suitable grieving period) than when married.

- In western culture the age sector over 55s has the highest divorce rate, and women are not rushing back to marriage.

- Recent information from the U.S. reveals depression as the No.1 emotional malady for retirees.

GOMs Unite!
What's wrong with it then?

Maybe there's nothing wrong with being a GOM!

It is your God-given right to be grumpy if that's what you want. You like the image of a lovable slob and grouse. You never wanted to be the life of the party, anyway. You're quiet and introverted and people have to accept that. There are lots of GOMs worse than you. You don't intend to change for anyone, especially your wife. You've brought in the income for 40 years, provided a good house, educated the kids, what else do you have to do?

You can pretend you're Walter Mattau, if you like, or Jack Lemmon. Now there's a couple of blokes who knew how to enjoy being GOMs. They made an art form out of it.

However if

· you can't see any reason for getting out of bed each morning, and

· you're asking the question "Is this all there is to life?", and

· you're feeling miserable or lonely or unwanted, then

Read this book.

It won't bite you. Get your score on the quiz and see how you compare with your mates.

Maybe you would be happier if you were more active, had some adventure, joined a local club, and considered the feelings of others rather than your own. But be careful! You might end up really enjoying life, but still with a quiet perspective. Maybe you won't be the life of the party, but at least you'll be enjoying the music.

Twelve Blokes who got Retirement Horribly Wrong

Lets begin by meeting twelve grumpy old men and seeing if there are ways of making them more satisfied with their lives

(The names have been changed to protect the guilty)

Bloke 1: Chris
Conspicuous Consumer (& Skite!)

Chris talks mostly about his wealth. Not directly, but indirectly. About his latest expensive purchase, the huge tax he has to pay, or the high cost of French wine. He knows full well that he has more money than most of his friends. He likes to describe other people as mean. He loves to show off his wealth but you suspect he's not all that generous.

Do you know someone like this ?

In spite of the thousands of ads on TV, in newspapers and magazines, which tell you that you won't be happy in retirement unless you have lots of money, it's simply not true.

Your financial advisor can tell you till the cows come home that you need more money to be safe and secure, but the fact is - happiness won't come from counting your money each day.

You can never have enough money by definition. However much you have, you'll always need a little more. A more luxurious car, a bigger boat, a more extensive wine cellar. But happiness in retirement doesn't work that way.

Conspicuous consumption will provide only a temporary thrill at the very best. Before the warranty has expired, the gloss will have faded. The advertising people will have won the battle, hands down.

> I'll never forget Chris
> God knows, I've tried

So what can you do if you're like Chris?

· You've got to learn to like yourself and your friends, even if they don't have much money or power or prestige.

· Friends can provide you with happiness, like nothing else.

· You've got to be active, because if you don't use it, you'll lose it.

· Learning something new every day will prevent boredom and stagnation.

· Do something for somebody less fortunate than yourself.

· Give your partner a pleasant surprise.

· Live every day as if it's your last.

Nobody promises you tomorrow. When you belly-ache about mowing the lawn, remember it's far better to be on top of the grass rather than underneath it.

"Contentment is...
not to love what we want but rather to want and appreciate what we have."
- The Dalai Lama

Bloke 2: Eric
The Obsessive Egotist

Eric talks only about himself. He has no interest in others. He is almost totally self-centred. If you talk about him or his children, he is interested, but if you mention other activities, or other people, he simply does not respond.

Are you at all like Eric?

Unfortunately there are lots of people like Eric. He needs help.

If you say to him "I poisoned my mother-in-law yesterday", his response will be "I poisoned some weeds". He has to relate everything back to himself.

He fails to see that after a short time no one wants to listen to him any more. He would have many more friends and be a lot happier if he appreciated other people's problems.

One good starting point is to help people who are less fortunate than you are.

> Blokes like Eric lack compassion.
> A visit to the children's ward at the hospital or an old people's home may help to broaden his horizon. Better than a visit to the pub or to the doctor!

So what can you do if you're like Eric?

- Offer assistance at the local respite centre, nursing or old people's home, or at the local hospital.

- If you are a handyman you could make wooden toys for sick children.

- If you like driving you could drive oldies to visit doctors and dentists, or shopping.

- Try giving a hand at Meals on Wheels.

- Read a book to an invalid neighbour once a week.

The biggest gain will be to you. Helping less fortunate folk will generate satisfaction and purpose and make your life much more worth while. Don't expect loads of gratitude, it may not come. But the gratitude will, none the less, be there.

Retirees doing volunteer community work are always happy people.

You will cease to believe you are simply sitting in God's waiting room, filling in time until you die. You will be far less bored, and far less boring. Far less self-centred.

> At least Eric won't ever be lonely,
> he enjoys his own company too much

# Bloke 3: Workaholic Wally
Moping for his Lost Prestige

Wally is bored. He cannot find anything to entertain him. He has few interests. He longs to be back at work. When he was at work he was someone.

Surely you're not like Wally?

Wally has never handled change well.

His environment has changed, but he doesn't see any need to change his lifestyle. He treats his house as though it were his office and his wife as though she were his secretary.

Retirement is vastly different from work, but Wally hasn't realized this yet.

His marriage didn't always work out as he expected, but since he was busy at work, he didn't see that as a problem. Perhaps they kept together for the sake of the children.

He thinks he has done his bit, but suddenly no one at work needs him any more.

> Wally has invented a labour saving device...
> It's called "Tomorrow"

So what can you do if you're like Wally?

· Professional counselling would be a start, but the problem needs to be identified first. Have a serious discussion with your partner about the opportunities that life offers.

· Above all else, you need friends. Forget about work.

· U3A, Probus, the golf club, the tennis club, the local choir could be good contacts.

· Get out, move on and meet new people.

· A new hobby or two would bring you into contact with others. French cooking lessons, stamp collecting, model boat building, cryptic crosswords, jigsaws.. anything!

· Maybe your wife has been too tolerant.

People are dying today who have never died before. Wally could well be next.
For all intents and purposes he has already died.

Bloke 4: Lenny
The Loafer

Lenny does nothing that can be avoided. He watches eight hours TV every day. He is leading a virtual life as seen in "soapies", talk shows and "reality TV". He seldom remembers what he saw. This allows him never to have to think for himself. Can't remember when he last read a book.

Nobody admits to watching this much TV because secretly they are ashamed of themselves.

Lenny is actually enjoying someone else's life rather than his own.

He laughs at the sit-coms, even when they repeat the same joke several times. He also laughs at the poor unfortunates who expose their personal problems on the talk shows.

His patient partner has given up trying to get him moving. Perhaps she thinks that at least he is not annoying her.

There is less to Lenny than meets the eye.

Each day he spends eight hours asleep, eight hours watching TV, and he wastes the rest.

All retired people need exercise. Certain exercises can be dangerous. But the most dangerous exercise, however, is sitting in a chair.

What can you do if you're like Lenny

· Switch off the TV, and plan your day away from the TV.

· Mark on the TV guide the "must see" programs, with a limit of two hours per day.

· Go to the local library one morning every week and start looking for books which might interest you. Get six or eight based on the blurb. Get both fiction and non-fiction.

· Don't expect to finish every book. If you don't like a book after twenty pages don't waste your time!

· Begin each day with a brisk walk of thirty minutes or more.

· Try to find some compatible friends, even if it is to discuss the soapies.

Bloke 5: Know-all Noel
Opinionated & Dogmatic

Noel gets very upset if you disagree with him. His opinion is correct. If you can't agree with him, then he considers there is something wrong with you. He loves to make dogmatic statements. Only disagree with him if you want an argument.

Of course you're not like Noel

Perhaps Noel feels he has never been recognized for his brilliance.

He would have achieved more but was never properly understood.

At work he was discriminated against, passed over for promotion.

Noel doesn't have many real friends. People tend to avoid him.

He would like to have lots more friends, and can't understand why he doesn't.

Perhaps he lacks self-esteem. But he tries to put on a good show.

Noel often exaggerates his achievements in order to gain friends or respect. He fails to see it has the reverse effect.

> Noel can't see that the problem is his. Other people cause the problem, not him. They simply fail to see that he is correct.

So what can you do if you're another Noel?

· Winning every argument won't win friends.

· Even one very good friend who loves you can slowly build your self-confidence.

· This is retirement, not work. Be prepared to lose the debate sometimes.

· Others' opinions don't have to coincide with yours.

· Inviting the opinion of others, rather than contradicting, will gain you much-needed friends.

· Everyone has different backgrounds and experiences. Rather than tell others they're wrong, enjoy the diversity of opinions, and question your own.

Noel, together with his partner should examine his problem and look at what is causing it (don't sweep it under the carpet). There is an excellent chance that his problem stems from the way in which his parents treated him in comparison with his siblings. He should eventually come to see that it's not the end of the world if he loses an argument or two.

Bloke 6: Vic
The Vexatious Victim

Vic has been very badly treated by everybody. He is a victim. He complains that no one likes him, or gives him a fair go. Even his own children avoid him.

Are you this way inclined?

Vic loves to tell you of his latest misfortune. He wallows in self-pity.

He likes to tell you how badly his own children treat him. They never phone.

Vic has very few friends. No one wants to listen any more.

He is so concerned with his own problems he doesn't even notice yours.

He admits to more medical problems than everyone else. Watch out! He'll describe his symptoms and his gory operations for hours, if you let him.

Vic's neighbour said to him,:
"The next time you go past my house, I'd appreciate it."

How can Vic, and you, if you're like him, increase your enjoyment of life?

· We need to feel gratitude for the things we have. Not concentrate on the things we don't have.

· You could begin by making a list of things for which you are grateful. They're many, and identifying them would be helpful.

· Others have problems too. Be interested in their problems, as well as your own.

· You need heaps more laughter in your life.

· Don't take yourself too seriously. Learn to accept your frailties and get on with living.

It's quite possible that envy played a large role in his childhood. His parents may have favoured or even doted on a brother or sister. He has never addressed his envy and never grown out of it.

 # Bloke 7: Chatterbox Charlie
Going on.. And on..

Charlie talks endlessly. He never stops. He just goes on and on. If you want to say something you have to talk over the top of him. You'll need to talk loud, real loud. He can talk about anything and everything. If he ever asks a question, he'll follow it with his own reply.

Do you sometimes talk too much?

There are lots of people like Charlie about.

The fact that he doesn't know what he's on about, doesn't deter him.

He is happy to repeat himself over and over.

If no one listens, he just looks for a new audience.

Physically he likes to trap you in a corner so you can't easily escape. He is a crushing bore.

> I don't normally forget a face, but in Charlie's case I'm happy to make an exception. Criticism rolls off Charlie like a duck's back.

If you're like Charlie, what can you do?

· Someone needs to tell Charlie he has a problem. This won't be easy. They may need to sticky-tape his mouth shut. And tell him that silence is golden.

· His partner has probably given up.

· Wouldn't it be good if someone made a tape recording of Charlie and then played it back to him?

· Of course he'd never speak to you again, and that has to be a good thing.

> If all else fails, avoid him

Bloke 8: Sam
The Sexist

Sam is a male chauvinist. To him, females are there to cook the meals, clean the house, do the shopping, washing and ironing, and have the children. He makes all the important decisions in the family. All financial matters are decided by him.

There are still many Sams about.

In spite of many years of female liberation there still remain lots of sexist male chauvinists.

Often they are copying the attitudes of their fathers.

If you asked Sam he probably wouldn't recognize male centred attitudes.

If you ask Sam's partner, she might say "A woman does what she has to". She is resigned to it.

Sam doesn't realize that a partnership of equals is a lot more fun.

Sam believes that women should be placed under a pedestal

What can you do if you're like Sam?

· Sam doesn't see he has a problem. Perhaps you don't either?

· Sam and his wife could change roles for a day. Sam could start with the cooking and the washing up, followed by cleaning the house.

· Reading some books on female liberation would be a good start.

· The local female librarian would provide some suitable book titles if asked.

· Sam should realize that his partner will probably be lots happier after he has died.

> Sam's fathers' attitude was tolerated in his day, but, thankfully the world has changed and so should Sam

Bloke 9: Frantic Fred
The Frenetic Mover

Fred can't slow down after retirement. Why should he? He has been going flat tack all his life. Fred sees no need to slow down now. This is how life is. When he drives on holiday he has to go 500 km every day. Any less and he is "wasting" time.

Can you slow down?

Let's face it. It's not easy to slow down after being in the fast lane for 40 years.

Go, go, go! It's in the genes and you just can't stop yourself.

Fred is happy to tell you he can drive non-stop from here to kingdom come.

What he can't do so easily is tell you what he saw on the way.

He also doesn't know what to do when he gets there.

Live each day as if it's your last. Soon enough it will be

What does Fred need to do?

· Get a hobby like gardening or building model planes or cooking.

· He needs to stop and smell the flowers.

· He needs to realize that he has the time, possibly for the first time in his life, to enjoy the trip, rather than strive for the achievement of the destination.

· His partner will be far happier if he stops frequently and considers the landscape.

· Look at the animals, the birds, the plants, the crops, the hills, the ranges, the trees.

· Talk to the locals, the farmers, who eat the local produce. Buy a punnet of strawberries or a box of field mushrooms. Get out of your comfort zone and do the unusual!

· In the country, stop in every village and walk the main street. Say g'day to the locals.

· You're retired. It doesn't matter if you take a few extra days.

· Live in the NOW, not in the future.

It's the journey that's important, not the destination

Bloke 10: Frank
The Fastidious Fuss-Pot

Frank is too fastidious. He is too fussy, too clean. Everything in the house has to be immaculate at all times. It drives his partner to distraction. This is often a complaint that females have, but males can have it just as bad. This habit leaves no time for the interesting things in life.

Whether it's Frank or Frances, this habit is emotionally numbing and mind-destroying for both partners

A house can be just too clean.

Work, (cleaning) expands to fill the time available to do it. There is always something that you can find that needs cleaning. Always something to wash and iron. Why not run around the house naked sometimes or play the licenced village idiot for once!

When cleaning always takes precedence over reading a book, or the newspaper, or chatting with friends, or listening to music, or a long walk, it's gone too far.

When you enter a fastidiously clean house you can bet the owners are boring. They don't have time for the richer things in life.

Remember, your mind and your emotions will wither if you don't feed and encourage them.

My house is so untidy that vandals broke in and did $200 of improvements. I make the beds, sweep the house and six months later I have to do it all again.

HE WAS A BLOKE WHO BROUGHT HAPPINESS WHEREVER HE LEFT!!

What can Frank and Frances do?

- Have a serious discussion about where their life is heading.

- Try to see that endlessly cleaning the house, the car or the caravan is time wasted.

- Set some goals in other areas such as hobbies, reading, sporting, social, helping others less fortunate.

- Start by setting times for cleaning. How about one hour a day!

- All other times to be kept clear for other activities.

- Chat with your best friends about what they do.

- Ask your children for their opinion.

- Make a weekly visit to the library, and bring home some books.

- Book into a weekly meditation class. Put on the brakes and slow down.

Spouses don't value their partners' housekeeping qualities. They hardly notice them at all. They do value companionship and having fun.

Bloke 11: Claude
The Cautious Conservative

Claude was pushed by controlling parents into a conservative, secure job. Claude was reliable. He seldom took risks. He was an accountant, or middle level manager, or senior clerk, or auditor. Claude was always responsible. Maybe his parents had a little too much influence over him.

Should Claude's life in retirement continue the same? No! No! No!

But there is a very good chance that it will.

He's been in the same mould for 40 years. He's grown accustomed to it. He doesn't particularly like it, and is often bored, but it's comfortable.

The creative and rebellious spark, which was in him in his youth, has been quenched.

But now it's different. Retirement should not, must not, be the same as the previous 40 years.

Opportunities abound. Let's learn to live. Let's open our eyes.

Once you have found your creative pathway you will never be bored again. Indeed you'll never have enough hours in each day. You'll have lots more friends too.

What should Claude do?

· Forget the past.

· Break the mold.

· Start to take risks. Do something outrageous and out of character. Buy some colourful clothes. Take a holiday to Timbuktu. Grow a ponytail.

· Never tell anyone what you used to do. Forget it. Re-invent yourself.

· Start to use the creative part of your brain instead of the analytical.

· Take up painting, pottery, lead-light glass making, wood turning, toy making, boat building, silver-work, weaving, raise alpacas or donkeys.

· Write your life story, a Mills and Boon love story, a one-act play, your retirement trip report, a TV sit-com script, or a romantic letter to your partner.

· Log onto the Internet and start researching something. Your ancestors, the wart hog, medieval English history, the Napoleonic wars, the history of flight.

· If the first or second creative path leads nowhere, try a different approach. Go and ask your friendly librarian.

Bloke 12: Gary
The Greedy Gourmand Fatso

Gary loves food and wine. Lavish meals every day. He thinks he is a gourmet. Maybe he's just greedy. He's overweight, and has numerous medical problems, but he never accepts that this is due to his high intake of food. Gary lives to eat, rather than eats to live.

Should Gary modify his lifestyle?

Only if he wants a long, happy and healthy life.

Obesity is a growing medical problem in all the developed world.

Gary loves to recount in great detail the wonderful food and wine he consumed yesterday.

> The best exercise to develop is to place your two hands on the table and push your chair back.

Are there any suggestions for Gary?

· Gary needs to find something, anything, that he feels more excited about than food. He needs a passion - sex, sport, gym, film, collecting stamps - anything but food.

· Food is great, but if it's your biggest interest, you're in trouble.

· Increasing your energy expenditure would be a good start. Start walking for at least thirty minutes, every day.

· Develop friends whose central interest is other than food.

· Replace your membership of the Beef and Burgundy Club for one at the golf club.

# What then should we do?
So We Don't Become GOMs

**No one thinks they are like any of the previous twelve Grumpy Old Men.
None of us can see our own faults.**

Perhaps if we ask wives or partners we'll get a far different viewpoint, one closer to the truth.

Boring, unhappy guys are a fact of life. Be brave enough to ask your partner if you're a GOM.

Did you know that on average widows are far more likely to be happy, than still married women. (Obviously, after an appropriate grieving period.)

If your partner was bored and unhappy most of the time, wouldn't you be happier without him/her? I know I would.

So, what can be done to make boring blokes happy?

Let's look at some of the issues...

Re-Invent Yourself
In Retirement the Rules Change

How to Re-invent Yourself
When you retire, the rules change, and so must you

If you try to achieve nothing, that's what you will achieve. Set some goals, like learn something new. Try a new sport. Make a few new friends. Do a good deed for somebody.

The value system that served you well at work is no longer appropriate. Try changing from focused achievement to compassionate friendship.

Retirement is nothing like work. If you want to be happy, you have to change, (this may not be easy).

Many of your skills and habits from work are not useful any more. Like blaming someone for mistakes.

You've gotta move on.

For a happy retirement you'll need a completely new set of objectives, activities, friends, and ways to relax.

What do you have to do ?

· Forget who you were. Especially your title.

· Recall your youth, and the things you used to long to do as a boy or young man. Get in there and do them now!

· Get down off your high horse.

· Don't be afraid to take risks.

· Don't be afraid to make a fool of yourself.

· Get interested in things you never had time for before.

· Joining new groups will provide not only new activities but also new friends. (See the pages on Activities, Adventures, Music and Learning).

· Stop reading the jobs ads.

· Don't even think about the pursuit of money.

· Set out to make new friends.

Your mental stimulation must come from within, not from the in-tray.

Make New Friends
Become More Sociable

So you've decided you want to make some new friends but are not sure where to start. Perhaps you have moved to a new district, you've retired, or have time on your hands.

The first step is to make contact with people

· Join several clubs (there are lots of clubs listed in the chapter on pre-retirement planning). When you go to the club meeting, introduce yourself and ask questions about the club. Offer to help in some way. Show some enthusiasm.

· Go walking every morning before breakfast. Go to local spots where others walk. Parks, beaches and river walks are my favourites. Maybe a walk just around your block is a good first start. Enjoy the scenery, the shrubs and the flowers.

So now, at least, you're near other folk. What next?

· Forget your own problems for a moment. Hold your head high, gain eye contact and greet others with a smile. Say a cheerful hello to people. Take a handsome dog with you as a conversation piece.

Happy people are more sociable, tolerant, creative, open, loving and forgiving

---

- Saying "Hi, great day", "Looks like rain", or "Parking is bad" may be hackneyed, but these casual greetings can break the ice. Local news can provide a topic for an introduction.

- You need to have a genuine interest in these people and in what makes them tick. For example, how long have they been in the district? This is not about you, this is about them.

- Open your inner door to a feeling of compassion and loving kindness. This will allow you to communicate with others. All human beings are just like you. You need a willingness to reach out. Ask about *their* day. Listen to *their* problems.

- But don't rush it! Take your time, but also make and take your opportunities.

Last, here are some Don'ts

- You won't meet new folk while watching TV.

- You won't meet new folk while driving the car.

- You won't meet new folk if you're **sitting down**.

So get up and get out!

Win Friends
.. You Can't Buy Them

The most important component of a happy retirement is friends.

A truly rich man is one with many friends.

You can't put a value on friends, you can't buy friends.

In good times or bad, friends will be there for you. Friends do things for each other, with no thought of repayment.

Friends bring happiness, laughter, joy, excitement, sometimes sorrow.

If friends cost you money, then they are not friends.

There is no pretense with friends. You can just be yourself.

You learn so much from friends, sometimes trivial, sometimes important.

One special friend, partner, spouse, soul-mate is a tremendous help in having a long and happy retirement.

If you are a bit of a grumpy hermit, force yourself to join the local walking group, table-tennis, or other social club, and take an interest in the members. Your partner, at least, will be very grateful.

Be nice to your friends. If it wasn't for them, you'd be a total stranger....

> Friendship is like a house built of playing cards. A lot of patient, considered, delicate work to build it up, and one sudden gust of hot air to destroy it.

Enjoy Friends
and Conversations

It's pretty obvious to most, that friendships are built through conversations.

Do you want more friends? If you answer No, you're probably a fibber, having yourself on. If you still answer No, then buy an empty book and keep a diary!

Do retired folk need more friends? Yes.

The friends from work may not be so appropriate now you've retired.

So, what can we do?

· Top of the list has to be learn to listen. I mean really listen. Hear the whole story, consider it and reflect on what it means.

· Ask a question about what has just been said.

· Don't reply, "I did this", or "We did that". Instead reply "So what did you do then?" or "Gosh, what happened after that?"

· Be interested in others, especially your close partner.

If people are house bricks then conversation is the mortar of life. The mortar can be considered the stuff that binds us together, or it can be the stuff that keeps us apart. Mortar does both, and so do conversations.
What we say, counts.

- Whatever your "friend's" current interest is, should become the topic of conversation. (If you want the person to be a friend).

- Your own particular current interest can wait a while.

- Don't disagree. Even when years of study and experience tell you that the person is wrong, you won't gain a friend by saying, "You're wrong".

- Everybody has a perfect right to his or her opinion, on whatever evidence satisfies them. This is retirement, you're not at work now. The rules have changed. You don't have to win arguments. Being right just doesn't matter.

- Look for and enjoy diversity of opinion. We are all very different.

- Don't trump the last story with a bigger and better one. It won't win friends.

> It's better to keep your mouth shut and be thought a fool, than open it and remove all doubt.

Coping With..
.. A Lack of Money and Status

In retirement money is no longer number 1.

Let's look at some words from the philosophers.

Fortunately for those lacking a large income, the essential ingredients of pleasure, however elusive, were not very expensive - Epicurus

Wealth is, of course, unlikely to ever make anyone miserable. But the crux of Epicurus's argument is that if we have money without friends, freedom and an analysed life, we will never be truly happy. And if we have them, but are missing a fortune, we will never be unhappy. - Alain de Botton

We don't need more money, we don't need greater success or fame, we don't need the perfect body or even the perfect mate - right now, at this very moment, we have a mind, which is all the basic equipment we need to achieve complete happiness - The Dalai Lama

Money won't buy friends or happiness. (It didn't buy your children's love.)

(Some comedian said, "If you don't have happiness, send out for it").

The cemeteries are full of people who thought that the world couldn't get along without them.

All those ads about superannuation and savings are no longer relevant. It's too late to worry about money now. Be ingenious. Think of how little you can get by on. You can't take it with you — There ain't no pockets in shrouds! Focus instead on having fun.

Expenditure greater than income, then you're grumpy.

Expenditure less than income, you will be happy.

The thrill of owning a new Mercedes will have gone a long time before the warranty has. (The ad man will have won again).

After retirement it should be: What's today's adventure?

· The happiest retiree will have lots of good friends.

· Status, title, and letters will have given away to first names. Tom, Dick and Harry is all you're going to get, and that's great.

· No one will ever ask, "How did you earn a crust?"

· Don't even think of returning to your old work place, it's changed. (Hopefully, so have you!) Let someone else fill your old shoes.

· If you've lost enthusiasm and excitement for life, then visit the local nursing home and look at what life has in store for you in a few short years. Ouch!

You have reached the pinnacle of serenity, when you are no longer obsessed with money, no longer crave compliments and no longer seek publicity.

If you can do this, then truly you are a philosopher of life. Like Diogenes in a barrel. When King Alexander the Great asked him what he could do for him, Diogenes replied: "Move. You're blocking the sunshine."

While you have the mindset that more money will bring you happiness, you'll never be happy.

Enjoy your own Company
Learn to be Happy

Learn to be happy in your own company (or your dog's company). If you are happy with your own company, others will be too.

Move on from the old hectic work environment. Seek a different, happier, fuller, but quieter lifestyle. March to a different drum.

Read books. They are wonderful company. You'll meet so many interesting and different people. Read every day.

Listen, Learn and Love.

Quiet times are golden. Treasure them. Don't waste your time yearning for celebrity and glamour, or envying others.

Slow down, meditate, give your wife a massage. Be grateful for what you have. Don't get miserable about the luxuries you don't have.

Slow down. Smell the roses - grow the roses! Learn the philosophy of fishing.

Be sensitive to the feelings of others. Try to like people. They may smell funny. So do you. It you're bored most of the time, others will find you boring, also. Get excited. This is the first day of the rest of your life.

Don't fret because you're not in the commercial fast lane. Opt for the Buddhist slow lane. The afternoon knows what the morning never suspected.

Be modest about your achievements. Others haven't had your good fortune. Every day admire something wonderful your friends have achieved. Life is temporary. There is no rewind button, and there are no rehearsals. Hurry, hurry, it's last days!

Go for it now! It's never too late. Go for it with all your heart and all your mind!

Enjoy every single moment of your life, it's unique and precious. And it will never come again.
Today is a gift. That's why it's called the present.

Coping With..
.. The Terrible Truth

Most of us grew up with the notion that the truth is very important. But so are people's feelings. Sometimes your 'truth' will hurt and upset people. Keep your 'truth' to yourself.

The rules have changed in retirement land. In day to day living, it is probably best to forget truth, and focus instead on love, forgiveness, tolerance and friendship.

You can question people aggressively on their experiences or beliefs, and this may give you some feeling of superiority or smugness. But it won't gain you friends. Especially in retirement, friends are gold.

Tolerate your friend's blind spots, as they tolerate yours.

Even when, from years of experience, you know the truth, don't force it on others. They don't want to know.

The truth can be very painful. Don't harp on it. Move on.

Sometimes we need a beautiful illusion to help us go on.

Look for the good in others. We've all made mistakes, and we don't want to be reminded of them.

Every time I hear the word "Truth", I reach for my revolver

If we ask for the opinions of others, they may consider us wise. If, on the other hand, we offer our opinions too frequently, they won't.

Replace the idea of "truth" with one of "perception". We may never agree about the truth of some matter, but we can easily agree that our perceptions are different.

I'm not suggesting that you tell lies, but a "white lie" may be the lesser of two evils.

Let people enjoy their areas of ignorance. It does them no harm.

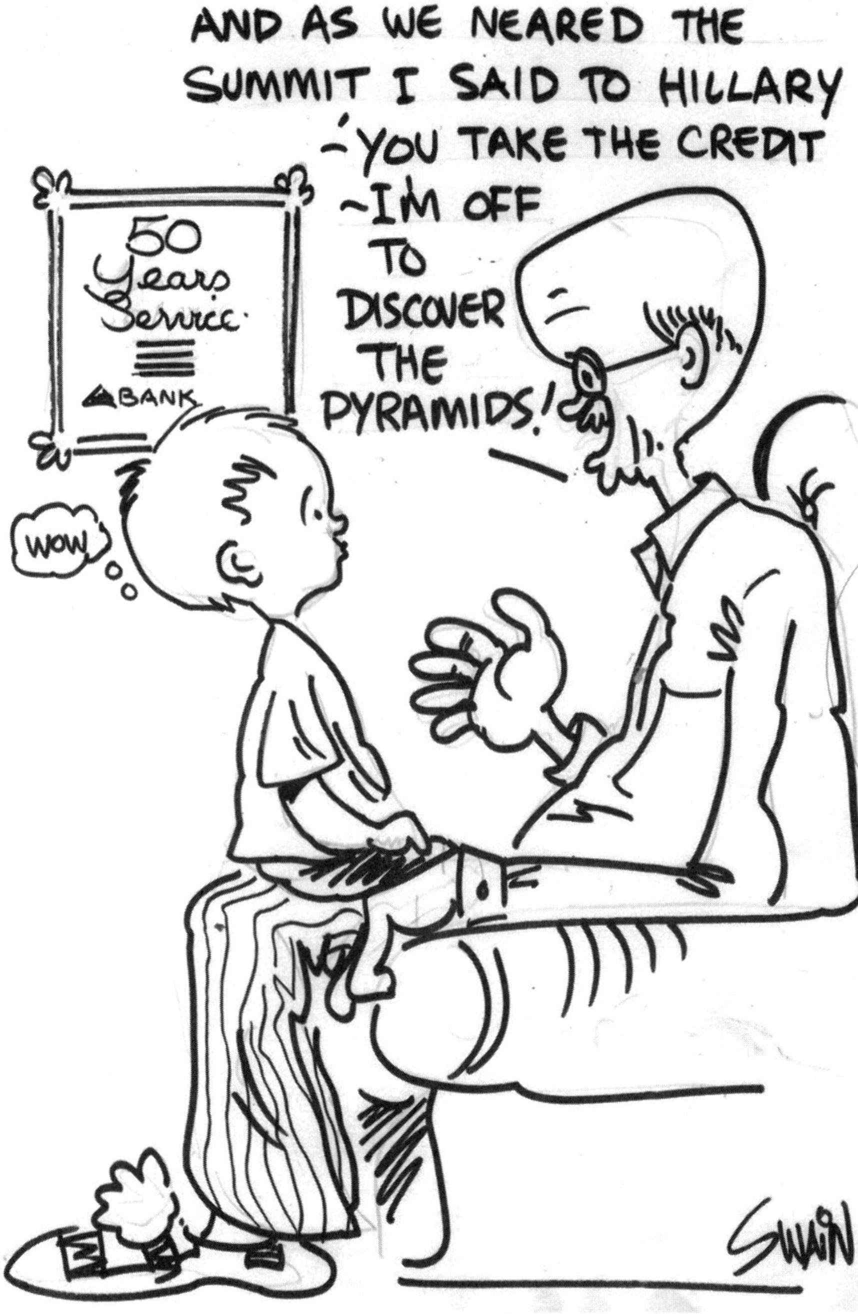
AND AS WE NEARED THE SUMMIT I SAID TO HILLARY - 'YOU TAKE THE CREDIT ~ I'M OFF TO DISCOVER THE PYRAMIDS!'
50 Years Service
BANK
WOW
SWAIN

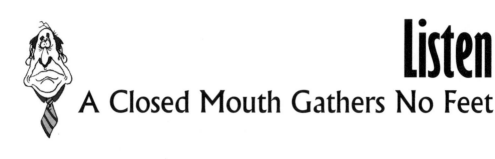

Listen
A Closed Mouth Gathers No Feet

Listening is never easy, and many retirees are not good at it.

- Most of us love to talk, and tell our own stories. (Who can blame us – it's much more fun.)

- If you are listening you may learn something. If you're talking you won't.

- Try "Active Listening". This is real listening, rather than thinking about what clever words with which to respond.

- Try focusing on what is being said, and ask a question relating to it.

- Two monologues don't make a dialogue. You need to listen.

- If you learn to listen attentively, you'll be less likely to be bored.

- Try to free yourself from any compulsion to disagree. Perhaps just ask polite questions. Even remark "That's interesting, I've never thought of it that way."

- You don't have to reply immediately. Allow a "moment of golden silence". Silence can do wonders in a conversation.

Every time I open my mouth some fool starts to talk

- Most of us look good until we open our mouths.

- If you really want to upset the person speaking don't look at him/her, gaze vacantly into the distance. (Then, everyone knows you are not listening.)

Even fish don't get into trouble if they keep their mouths shut

---

Angry people don't listen. If you listen, you may be more relaxed

Enjoy Music
The Universal Language

Music is unique and it deserves your close attention.
It can do so much for you.

Before I retired I never imagined that music would play such an important role in my retirement. But it has. It has enriched my life considerably. There are lots of ways to include music in your retirement.

· Join a choir or singing group. Some of these groups sing serious music whilst others sing light classical or pop. Then there are amateur productions of musical comedies looking for singers. It can be great fun. You'll make new friends, too.

· Learn to play a musical instrument. It's not hard or expensive, and worth a try. Electronic keyboards are very popular, with simple music to follow. (But one bit of advice, don't buy a second hand keyboard. With advances in modern technology, they are becoming cheaper with time, and older models can't be repaired). Harmonicas are simple and cheap and can produce excellent music. Second hand button accordions are cheap and easy to play. A recorder or tin whistle is easy to play and are fun. If starting out, choose an instrument that plays only the tune, (no base) it's easier to get results. Alternatively, guitars are very popular, and you can play either tunes or chords. Buy a cheaper instrument first, and if all

---

Only two instruments sound worse than an accordion:
Two accordions

---

goes well, sell it after 12 months, and buy a better one. Join the local musical group to gain encouragement. You'll find them very supportive.

· Listening to music you like is an excellent way to start. Try the radio first. When I retired I'd never heard of Folk Music Festivals. Now I've been to most in Australia and they're great fun. Country Music Festivals are also very popular. These mostly feature guitars, while folk festivals encompass a hundred different instruments, from flutes and violins to harps and accordions. There are also festivals of jazz, blues, Celtic and world music.

· Music appreciation groups are also popular these days. They range from opera and jazz, to classical music. It's a great way to hear good music of your choice and meet new friends with similar interests.

· If you gain a moderate degree of competence in playing or singing you can get great satisfaction from entertaining at nursing homes and retirement villages. You can go from depressed to being very popular, in a relatively short time. Music is the last thing that we retain as our memories age and fade.

One of the great aspects of music is the spiritual feeling of wellbeing it can generate. It can be both very relaxing and soothing. There is appropriate music for every mood.

I have never seen a consistently happier group of people than one singing together or playing instrumental music together. Everyone contributes joyously and smiling, and no one is arguing. If you play a bum note, no one notices. Quite often you don't even know who the other musicians are, or what language they speak. It really doesn't matter. It's magic!

Learn Something New
Every Day

Learning for the brain is what exercise is to the body.

· Research shows that learning, whatever the subject, will not only be beneficial to your brain, but also to your physical well-being. That's great news.

· Learning is so very absorbing that you'll forget it's time to eat.

· Pick a project or an author. Write a report (or at least brief notes) on what you have learned.

· You will be far less bored and far more interesting to be with.

· The world is a wondrous place to explore. Start in your local library. Modern library catalogues are very easy to navigate. You can choose what turns you on (NOT what the teacher made you do). Astronomy, dinosaurs, mammals, primates, volcanoes, Islam, Buddhism, water resources, Roman history, etc.

· Make the local library your second home (rather than the pub or club). You'll find librarians are such helpful people. Simply tell them what subject you're interested in. They'll point the way.

Those who think they know it all upset those of us who do!

- You'll be far happier, your partner will be a lot happier, and you'll have more friends.

- If you have stopped learning, you might as well be dead.

- But, don't show off your recent knowledge, hide it in your pocket.

You're currently using between 10% and 20% of your brain, so it's unlikely you'll overload it.

Enjoy Leisure
It Won't Kill You

Leisure time in our daily routine is always welcome

It may seem a little strange to include a section on leisure but some retirees seem so hell bent on frenetic activity there is simply no time for leisure. They're late for every function, and then have to leave early to get to the next one.

- Leisure time is not just simply watching TV, although that is okay some of the day.

- Quiet times of complete relaxation and meditation add a richness to the active part of the day. A time to think and ponder.

- Give your partner a (no-payback) massage.

- Take a slow walk through a park or along a river bank, perhaps at the end of a hectic day. Feel close to the trees, the river, the dogs, the cats, the birds, the children. Take time to smell the roses.

- Look for a quiet, non-violent, feel-good, thoughtful movie. (If you can find one.)

The past is history, the future is a mystery

- Read to your partner a good book or some poetry.

- Learn to slow down, relax, and enjoy your own company, or that of your dog. Find some serenity in your quiet times.

- Think about what your friends are doing. Write a letter to an absent colleague.

- Keep a diary or journal.

Break Out..
.. Of Your Prison of Sloth

Use It or Lose It. Don't be a Couch-Potato

TV, computers, remote controllers, and other labour-saving devices have given us a problem. It's just too easy to get through life with little regular physical activity. Our affluence is such that regular physical activity has to be planned into our lives. Strangely enough, many of us find it difficult to find the time to exercise. The so-called labour-saving devices have theoretically given us more free time in which to exercise, but we live in a prison of sloth. We have to do a jail break.

Regular physical exercise can:

- lower blood pressure

- improve weight control

- reduce the likelihood of stroke and heart attack

- reduce depression

- improve your sleep, and lots more.

A woman was asked if her husband did any exercise.
She replied "Well, he was out last week, five nights running."
Her husband claimed he was in shape... "Round is a shape."

Walking is the easiest, cheapest, and one of the most effective ways of gaining your daily exercise. How about you walk every day for at least thirty or forty minutes!

Walking is more fun with a mate. Someone to encourage you to go, someone to talk to. Another opportunity to build a friendship. The time will pass very quickly if you talk as you walk. Look at the birds, also the ones without feathers, and the bees, the flowers and the trees. Walk through a park, along a riverbank, around a lake, somewhere that is pleasing to the senses. Say hello to strangers as you go.

There are literally hundreds of sporting clubs to consider. Not only do you get fun and exercise and the adrenalin pumping, but you make new friends, and that's a good thing. Table tennis, badminton, dancing, volleyball, weight training and billiards are great indoor sports, while golf, swimming, tennis, croquet, petanque, bush walking, kayaking, surfing, cycling, lawn bowls, athletics, horse riding, fishing, jogging, archery, and shooting, are all outdoor. There is nothing quite so pleasant as a hot shower, a cool drink and a reminisce with your mates after a tiring game.

If you want to grow younger, you might try thinking, acting, and behaving like a younger person. Straighten up! Hold your head high, throw your chest out, and pull in your chin. Don't shuffle. Pick up your feet and stride. Right away you have eliminated years from your appearance and even more from your behaviour.

If you want to get fat and die soon, just stay sitting in your favourite TV armchair

Have an Adventure
Each Day

Live every day as if it's your last.
One day it will be.

You don't have to climb Mt. Everest (though that's not a bad idea) to have an adventure, and you don't need a fortune. Meeting a child or a dog or talking to a fisherman or asking for reading advice from a librarian – all these things can be little adventures. What you need is an unprejudiced mind. Retired life will be much richer and happier if you get out of your comfort zone occasionally, and take some risks. You need to be open to life's unexpected and unplanned incidents. Here are a few.

- Climb a local mountain.

- Go hot air ballooning.

- Give abseiling a go. (It's better than falling off the perch.)

- Buy a metal detector and go find your fortune.

- Paint a picture by numbers.

- Learn how to throw a cast net for bait. (You'll catch all sorts of strange things, including the interest of passers by, and cause lots of laughs.)

An adventure a day keeps the doctor away

- Go to an observatory one night and learn about the stars.

- Join the National Park walking and camping group.

- Take an off-shore fishing trip.

- Have a lesson in gliding.

- Go on the Great Australian Bike Ride. (Your local cycle store has the details.)

- Buy a kayak and explore rivers, lakes and lagoons. The bird life is wonderful.

- Hire a jet ski.

- Talk to strangers, especially if they look different from the norm.

- Take a day sail on a 70ft yacht and take the wheel for an hour.

- Write a Mills and Boon novel.

- On a breezy day hire a catamaran and get the adrenaline pumping.

- Take a camel ride.

- Take an overnight horse trek where you camp out and hear bush yarns.

- Go for a trek where a donkey is used to carry your food and gear.

- Catch a barramundi. (It took 12 month's planning before I finally caught one. I had to throw back a 5 pounder because it was too small! My wife was delighted to keep her 16 pounder.)

- Shoot the rapids in large inflatable rubber raft. Be prepared to get wet.

- Take a berth on a cargo ship, say Cairns to Thursday Island and return. (It's great.)

- Trade your wheels on a campervan and circle Australia (take at least 12 months.). Take a volume of Banjo Patterson along and read some every evening.

- Have a week in a remote fishing camp in the Northern Territory. — Don't forget the Aeroguard!

- Hire a 4WD and basic camping gear, drive along a remote beach and camp out under the stars. (Take a bag of firewood for the camp fire. A license may be required.)

- Found a TV discussion group.

- On Australia day cook corned beef and damper over an open fire for your friends.

- Join a few clubs. Force yourself to be sociable. Play a few sports with mates

Cheer up your Wife
It's Her Retirement Too!

You're no longer the boss, you're an equal partner.

· Ask your wife or partner, now that you've finally retired, what does **she** want to do.

· For forty years she has provided the base camp platform for you to strut your stuff. Now it's her turn. It's her retirement too!

· Ask your wife or partner to write down the ten tasks she hates to do, and you volunteer to do them, or get someone else to do them.

· Ask her to write down the ten activities she would love to do. (I hope the first is not to get a divorce.) Tell her you will do your utmost to see she can achieve all of these.

· She has done the "good mother" thing for all these years, and now deserves more adventure, more freedom, and perhaps less of her husband asking what's for dinner. (How about you being the chef tonight!)

After all, the biggest problem and often the only problem that wives have, is their husbands.

- Don't be a bad smell under your partner's feet. Don't talk endlessly about your last golf round. (Boy, is that boring!), or your arthritis. (She'll be happier, if you're busier.)

- Once a day, sit down next to your partner, with no TV or radio on, and talk with her. But most importantly, listen to her. Listen to her problems, but don't try to solve them. (I know that was what you did at work for the last 40 years, but retirement is different.) Just try to understand where she is coming from. She doesn't want you to solve her worries. She just wants a sympathetic ear.

Help Others
Help Those Less Fortunate

If you are not getting much satisfaction from life, then helping those less fortunate may fill the gap.

- You'll be a lot happier if you replace worrying about your investments, with helping others who are down and out.

- Perhaps you could start by trying to be the best neighbour in the street. (Surprise those who thought you were a GOM.)

- Don't help others if what you are really after is to get something back in return. The reward is solely in the doing.

- Don't wait for thanks. Often, other people have just too many problems to get around to it.

- The bulk of charity work is done by retired folk.

- Every charity, old persons' home and respite centre that I know of, can always use more volunteers. Try Meals on Wheels, St. Vincent de Paul, Red Cross, Friends of the Hospital, etc.

You'll make a lot of real friends and have heaps of fun.

Charity workers are among the happiest people in the world

Soul-Mates..

.. And Why You Need One

One of the strongest factors in leading a long and happy retired life is a soul-mate or very close partner.

- A soul-mate is someone with whom you can really share the joys and sorrows of life's ups and down.

- A soul-mate is someone to whom you can tell your innermost secrets and anxieties too, and who will put up with you when you're having a very bad day.

- If it's your wife or long term partner, she has probably done the good mother bit for a lifetime. Now she deserves more adventure and freedom. Help her to find it.

- Occasionally we'll make an unfortunate statement and cause someone real hurt, maybe without even knowing. A soul-mate will be the only one to love you sufficiently to tell you. So listen.

- If your soul-mate disappoints you sometimes, look in the mirror and see what she has to put up with.

- If you don't have a soul-mate, go looking for one. Join clubs while you search.

Having or being a soul-mate gives you a new challenge every day.
Never take it for granted

Why Can't Women
Be More Like Men?

It just may be that one of the influences that turn retirees into GOMs is the role some females play. Heaven forbid!

Unfortunately, not all women are saints. If your husband is a GOM maybe he is just what you deserve. This should not be overemphasized, but also, it should not be entirely overlooked. You've trained him wrong!

Wives, if you don't want your husband to be a GOM, then there are activities that could best be avoided.

· Getting too obsessed with household cleaning. Go see a movie together and let the dust settle.

· Getting stuck in mind-numbingly boring daily routines. Don't be task-oriented. be emotionally oriented towards your partner and family.

· Nagging and complaining over smaller and smaller issues.

· Being obsessed with your career.

· Being always on the go, go, go!

> You may think that you are trying to solve your husband's problems, but at least make certain you're not the problem.

And there are activities that could be considered more often, providing a better balance, such as.

- · Some adventure and excitement.

- · Complete relaxation with your partner.

- · Reading a book your partner has mentioned, so later, you can discuss it together.

- · Be prepared to show some gratitude for the good things your husband does.

- · Check that you are not creating superfluous work, when you should be enthusiastic about having some fun.

Don't be a Crude Slob
Good Manners Cost Nothing

It doesn't make you more macho!
And guess what? — Women hate it.

In their desire to appear very macho, some men seem to cultivate bad manners. Such habits, rather than attracting friends, lose them. These include:

· Swearing and profaning.

· Telling off-colour jokes in mixed company.

· Making disparaging remarks about your wife and her friends.

· Being racist about immigrants and Aborigines.

· Being judgmental and criticising others.

· Burping, belching and passing wind.

· Drawing attention to yourself with uncouth remarks.

Wally said there were two groups he couldn't stand:
Racists and Japanese

**The best joke you can ever tell is one against yourself.
No one will be offended.**

Retirees need stacks of friends, both male and female, and good manners will help you gain them.

Let your wife find her Prince Charming again.

The Body is Aging
How to Live With it

The most important thing is your attitude. Here you have a choice, and the choice is critical.

By the time we reach retirement age we know that our aging body is starting to let us down. It doesn't work the way it did at age 20 or 30. We will have witnessed a number of friends suffer from serious and terminal illnesses. How can we cope?

Let's assume that you are receiving the best possible medical care to reduce the symptoms and the pain, and you have the physical assistance to make life as easy as possible. What else can you do?

Some people look on the sunny side of life and are grateful for what they do have. We all know such people. They tend not to talk of their own problems. They talk happily about what they can still enjoy. If their problems are spoken of, they make light of them, even joke about them. Such people are an inspiration for us, for they show us the way to cope when our turn comes.

Other people, however, can only whine and moan. Why me? The only topic of conversation is their problems. Whatever the topic of discussion they manage to swing the subject around to how bad things are for them.

> I was surprised by the ever-cheerful attitude of a terminally ill friend with lung cancer, so I asked his wife, "What's he like when he's by himself?"
> She replied, "I don't know, I've never been with him when he's by himself."

Attitude is the key word. At a time when friends are more important than ever, your attitude to your frail body will determine your friends and consequently your happiness.

Most of the work of the world is done by people who are not entirely well. You, too, can enjoy life even when less than 100% well. Fight the good fight if you fall sick.

Watch TV Actively
Enjoy it More

Generally speaking, watching TV has to be one of the most passive things we can do. Most of the time we absorb the material like a sponge. But it doesn't have to be so. You can enjoy the experience and gain much more from the programs, (some programs at least), by "watching actively".

· Pretend that you are a reviewer. Keep a notebook and pencil by your TV chair.

· When the promo is presented, note what they claim about the program. Most promos make all sorts of wild claims. "This program will change your whole life!" etc.)

· Then when the program is run, compare your expectations with the reality. Ask yourself, "Was your whole life changed?" Write down the omissions and downright lies and send your comments off to the TV station.

· Most dramas and soapies are ripe for criticism. Give them marks out of ten for plot, acting, dialogue, music, scenery, and anything that takes your fancy. If the plot is paper thin or over-full with melodrama and agony aunts, write this in your review.

> The technology of modern TV is very good, but the program content often leaves a lot to be desired. Let the broadcasters know.
> You will learn a lot in the process and become a far more interesting person. For a start, you will be able to remember what you watched last night.

· Don't just say "crap", and throw a rock at the TV, let the station know why the program is rubbish. If the doco or film was fantastic, write and say so. Write letters to the editor. Aim to get read out on feedback programs on the ABC.

· Start up a little informal group called TV and Film Discussion Club. Agree to watch the same program sometimes and give each person five minutes to say what was good, what was bad, and why.

The A-Z of Retirement

Attitude to retirement is far more important than money.

Try to discover some little **A**dventure every day.

If I am **A**ngry I don't listen. Try to listen, and be happier.

Baggage from the past is best discarded. (Lighten up your load.)

If you're **B**ored and **B**oring try cheering up a friend.

Compassionate attitudes foster good friendships. You won't have buddies if you "know it all".

Don't just sit alone in your room, life is a **C**abaret, Old **C**hum.

If you have a **C**hip on your shoulder, have one on both sides so you're balanced.

This is my A-Z
How about you write your own A-Z in the spaces left vacant

Dare to be different! Grow old **D**isgracefully!

Diversity of personalities and opinions makes the world a richer place. Appreciate the views of others.

You'll lose your pals with **D**ogmatic statements.

This is the first **D**ay of the rest of your life. Make it unique. Walk a new path.

Keep a **D**iary. (Write **D**aring things in it.)

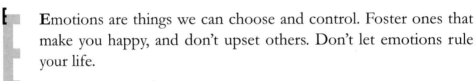

Emotions are things we can choose and control. Foster ones that make you happy, and don't upset others. Don't let emotions rule your life.

Envy is a wasted emotion. **E**xcitement brings us to life.

Enthusiasm is the best emotion that we have. Never be embarrassed to be enthusiastic.

Enjoy your daily **E**xercise. Feel good about it and you'll glow!

Eat wisely. You are what you eat!

Friends, **F**itness and **F**un are what you're aiming for in a happy retirement.

Forgiveness brings us out of the past, and into the present, and gives us **F**reedom.

Do not go **G**entle into that **G**ood night.

God give me the patience to accept what I must, the determination to change what I can, and the wisdom to decide which is which.

Gratitude for what you have is great. It will blow away your **G**rumpiness.

Your **G**arden can be one of your best friends. Lose yourself there.

Help others less fortunate. (Be sympathetic and caring.)

Humility wins brownie points.

Intellectual pursuits reduce memory loss, and improve your health.

Impatience and **I**ntolerance are your worst enemies. (Kill them off.)

Be **I**nterested in others. (Try to work out how they tick!)

Judgement of others is never wise. Try to wonder why people act like they do.

Jealousy is another wasted emotion.

Justice is admirable. (But not universal.) Accept that life doesn't always go your way.

 "**K**now thyself"! An unexamined life is not worth living.

Kindness to others is its own reward. It also brings out the best in our friends.

 Love, **L**eisure, **L**aughing and **L**earning are what you need for a happy retirement.

Listening is a virtue. Don't offer unsolicited advice.

Libraries are full of wonder and excitement. An excellent second home.

Winning the **L**ove and approval of everybody is highly unlikely, so accept this. Accept yourself, complete with **L**imitations and foibles.

 **M**aterialism and **M**oney are unlikely to bring you happiness. More **M**usic might.

 Now is the time to make peace with your enemies. Don't delay until it's too late.

Now is the time to get out of the house and do something. Anything!

Others have **O**pinions. Respect these.

 Your **P**erceptions are your own, and nothing more. They may be correct, but who knows, they just may be wrong.

Physical activity should be an everyday feature of your life. Get out and enjoy!

Poke some fun at yourself. Don't be a "Stick in the Mud".

 **Q**uestioning other people's actions is, unfortunately, a very human trait. Don't feel that you have a calling to change other people.

 Never nurse **R**esentment. It is your second worst enemy. (Let it die.)

Take a **R**isk. Be a devil. Get outside your comfort zone. Let the unexpected happen. **R**elish every little encounter.

 A **S**oul-mate is a very desirable **S**olace and comfort.

Self-interest won't gain you friends.

Sloth is your third worst enemy. So is **S**troppiness.

Truth in all matters sounds grand. But it's good to remember no one has a licence to inflict cruel truth on others.

If you think you are **T**reated badly by everybody, this should ring alarm bells in your head about yourself.

Talk to complete strangers. (The stranger the better.)

Use it or lose it!

Unselfishness and generosity are admirable traits. (Use them to excess.)

Unhappiness can be overcome with good friends, and a generous heart.

Have a **V**ision of what you want to do before you die.

Don't be a **V**ictim. Sometimes it is easier to see ourselves as victims rather than as accountable adults. We blame our poor choices or failed endeavours on an unhappy childhood, on cultural oppression, on class, on prejudice, or on society in general. Don't blame anyone. Just get on with it and have a go!

Wisdom can come from anyone, rich or poor, famous or unknown. Don't think you know it all. Look for it in the most unlikely places.

Don't make your unhappy **W**ife a happy **W**idow. Appreciate your wife. She's been a partner in your success.

It ain't no triumph to **W**in an argument. Better to win a friend.

Don't be frightened to be **X**-cited and **X**-uberant. Just because you are old, you don't have to be glum. Be gutsy! Don't take yourself too seriously. Being an old sour-puss is no laughing matter.

Youth was wonderful, but tempestuous and unstable. Retirement can be much more lucid and serene.

Zealous persons, uncompromising and fanatical, won't have many friends.

Those with **Z**est for life will have friends all around them.

# Pre-Retirement Planning
Plan for Tomorrow

What will I do, when I have no office to go to?

When considering retirement you can't start too early to make plans. The three key attributes for success are flexibility, adaptability and creativity. Set about planning to re-invent yourself to have heaps of fun. Replace the words "can't" and "won't" with the words "I'll give it a go". You've nothing to lose and everything to gain. (You'll have to let go of your current title, position and self-importance.)

With lots more free time you'll need heaps more friends. People you've never met before, but ones who have similar interests. The best way of doing this is to make a list of all the clubs and groups and associations which you can join. Here are some.

· U3A (University of the 3rd Age, may be the first port of call.)

· Book discussion group (Enquire at your local library)

· Probus

· Bush Walking Club

· Over 60s Holiday and Travel Club

> There's no use just sitting alone in your room,
> Come hear the music play,
> Life is a Cabaret, old chum,
> Come to the Cabaret.

- The Caravaners' Association

- A Political Party

- The Local Rate Payers Association (Help plan the future.)

- A Service Club (Rotary, Lions etc.) Meet like-minded folk and work for the community.

- The Movie Appreciation Club

- The Exotic Plants Club (Orchids, Roses, Bonsai, etc.)

- The 4 Wheel Drive Club

- The Local Historical Group (Maybe research your own family.)

- The Yoga Group

- The Music Appreciation Group (jazz, classical, blues, folk, etc.)

- The Computer Users' Group (digital photography is all the go.)

- A Church Social Club

- A Bridge Club

Then there are Art and Craft Groups.

- Painting (oils, watercolour, acrylic, etc.)

- Pottery

- Writing (There are lots of writing groups about, it's very popular.)

- Wood Working and Toy Making

- Boat and Model Building

- Sewing

- Cooking (Maybe Asian, French or Italian.)

- The Local Orchestra, Band or Folk Club

- The Choral Society or Church Choir

- The Local Drama Group

- The Debating Group

Then there are sporting interests to consider.

- Golf (The Veterans are a very happy group, and not too competitive. They are very happy to be above the grass still.)

- Tennis

- Bowls (Be warned, more people die playing bowls than any other sport.)

- Badminton (At your age I'd give squash a miss.)

- Croquet

- Petanque (A very sociable and skillful game.)

- Fishing (A great time to meditate)

- Table Tennis

- Dancing (line, tap, clog, belly, square, folk, etc.)

- Senior Athletics and Swimming

- The Local Gymnasium

- The Gliding Club

- Kayaking and Canoe Club

- Surfing

- Archery (You've got a new target now)

- Coach a junior sports team or be an official at the surf club.

Then there are heaps of lectures available from TAFE, universities, church groups and the U3A, on literally hundreds of subjects. If you can't tick at least a dozen topics for trial then don't retire. You're not ready for the biggest change in your life.

Plan for tomorrow, but live for today

Depression
And the Retired Man

Why some retired men become depressed

- They have lost their status, their title and authority.

- They have little to look forward to. Their life, as they see it, is behind them.

- "Is this all life has to offer?" is a common thought. "Why Bother?"

- Physical ailments are becoming more of a nagging problem

- Erotic allure and sporting prowess are out the window. What's left?

If you or your partner are depressed then what can you do? It's not going to be easy but there are steps that may help.

Changing a person's physical activities will eventually lead to a change in his mindset. If you want to change a man's attitude, first change his daily habits.

Practical steps towards defeating depression

- Face up to your problems and discuss them **fully** with your doctor, soul-mate or partner. Don't ignore what is worrying you, address it.

- Only **you** can determine if you wish to be happy or depressed. It's like losing fat, you really have to work at it.

- Replace those constant obsessive and self-pitying thoughts about yourself with thoughts about others. Particularly others who are less fortunate than yourself.

- **A circuit breaker is required. Something physical is best.** Talking to and helping others with disabilities or those in unfortunate circumstances is excellent.

- Start off by volunteering at the local nursing home, respite centre, old person's home, children's ward at the hospital, palliative care centre etc, where you come into contact with these people.

- If you can become a genuine care-giver, your mind will begin to focus on other people with bigger problems than yours. In addition, when you have free time, you will be far more likely to make constructive use of it, rather than indulge in self-pity.

ONCE 541,000
PEOPLE OBEYED
MY EVERY COMMAND
~TODAY IT'S
DIFFICULT TO
GET A
PLUMBER TO
DO WHAT
I WANT!!
SWAIN

Help to get Going
Don't be Embarrassed to Ask

All pride will do is make you lonely.

- Ask your wife if you are a GOM. (Grumpy Old Man). Ask her what is the first step you can take towards getting more out of life in retirement.

- Ask your wife what new activities and leisure interests you might take up. What subject you could study.

- Ask your children the same questions. After all, they know you better than most.

- Visit your friends and see how they cope. Ask them to help you join a club. (There are millions.)

- Contact a local lifestyle trainer, and ask for advice. (But some trainers may not be skilled in the challenges that many face after retirement).

- Contact Australia's 1st "Retirement School" Director, Jennifer Ballard, from Vision Life Coaching, ph 0413 586 125, or visit them online at www.visionlifecoaching.com.au Jennifer can assist in recognizing your retirement strengths and weaknesses and crystallize your retirement dreams and plans.

A Fulfilling Retirement
10 Reasons Why It Can Be

· For the first time in your life you are free to do whatever you want. Discover your suffocated inner self.

· No one is telling you what you have to do or how quickly you have to do it. Invent your own day, every day.

· You can go to bed as late as you like, and sleep in as late as you like. No need to set the alarm clock.

· You can indulge in your passion, whatever it is.

· You can help your partner realise her ambitions. Do you even know what they are?

· You can travel almost anywhere you want to go. (I've heard of people travelling round Australia on their old age pension!)

· Boring work-based reading can be replaced with reading for curiosity, adventure, pleasure and awe.

· Friends are entirely of your choosing and not necessarily work-related.

· You now have time to exercise regularly, play more sport and get fit and healthy. No longer are you wasting the best years of your life staring at a computer screen, getting round-shouldered and obese.

· Art, culture, handicrafts and hobbies can all now play a far greater part in your everyday life. Set your creative self free!

A Message From the Pro's
Philosophers Have Their Say

If there is any wisdom in this book it has probably come from the philosophers, both new and long ago. Here are some examples that I have found helpful.

Epicurus

"Fortunately for those lacking a large income, the essential ingredients of pleasure, however elusive, were not very expensive.

"Send me a pot of cheese, so that I may have a feast whenever I like." Such were the simple, inexpensive tastes of a man who had described pleasure as the purpose of life.

"Of all the things that wisdom provides to help one live one's entire life in happiness, the greatest by far is the possession of friendship".

Alain de Botton

"Wealth is, of course, unlikely to ever make anyone miserable. But the crux of Epicurus's argument is that if we have money without friends, freedom and an analysed life, we will never be truly happy. And if we have them, but are missing a fortune, we will never be unhappy."

Marcus Aurelius

"The perfection of character consists in living each day as if it were the last, and being neither violently excited, nor apathetic, nor insincere.

"Most men never find happiness anywhere; not in logical thought, not in wealth, not in fame, not in self-indulgence – nowhere."

Cicero

" Friendship by its nature admits of no feigning, no pretence; As far as it goes it is both genuine and spontaneous.

Margaret Olley

"Hurry, hurry, it's last days."

Deepak Chopra

Deepak lists, among others, the following factors for a long and happy life:

- Eat frugally

- Exercise and get plenty of fresh air

- Develop a placid and easy going personality

- Maintain a high level of personal hygiene

Stephan Grellet

"I expect to pass through this world but once; any good thing therefore that I can do, or any kindness that I can show to any fellow-creature, let me do it now; let me not defer or neglect it, for I shall not pass this way again."

Retired US General Norman Schwarzkopf in 1991,

"Six months ago 541,000 people obeyed a single command I gave. Today, it's even difficult to get a plumber to do what I want."

Sir Richard Steele

"Reading is to the mind what exercise is to the body."

Stephanie Dowrick

"Retirees involved in community service on a voluntary basis are one of our most contented groups".

Bertrand Russell

"Next to worry probably one of the most potent causes of unhappiness is envy. Instead of deriving pleasure from what he has, man derives pain from what others have. Whoever wishes to increase human happiness must wish to increase admiration and to diminish envy. The child who finds a brother or sister preferred before himself acquires the habit of envy, and when he goes out into the world looks for injustices of which he is the victim, perceives them if they occur, and imagines them if they do not.

"The root of unhappiness springs from too much emphasis upon competitive success as the main source of happiness.

"An expansive and generous attitude towards other people not only gives happiness to others, but is an immense source of happiness to its possessor, since it causes him to be generally liked.

"To be able to fill leisure intelligently is the last product of civilisation, and at present very few people have reached this level. The boredom that a man feels when he is doing necessary though uninteresting work is as nothing in comparison with the boredom that he feels when he has nothing to do with his days."

The Dalai Lama

"Unhappy people tend to be the most self-focused and are often socially withdrawn, brooding, and even antagonistic. Happy people are found to be more sociable, flexible, and creative and are able to tolerate life's daily frustrations more easily than unhappy people.

"Contentment is not to have what we want but rather to want and appreciate what we have."

"If you maintain a feeling of compassion, loving kindness, then something automatically opens your inner door. Through that, you can communicate much more easily with other people. And that feeling of warmth creates a kind of openness. You'll find that all human beings are just like you, so you'll be able to relate to them more easily."

I Did it My Way
A Personal Experience

My wife and I couldn't wait to do the grand trip of Europe on retirement. We had, in younger days, enjoyed a six-week tour of France and Germany but now we had at least four months, and no children. With hired car, small tent and air-beds we caught the English channel ferry and headed south to the Central Massif of France. Clement Ferand was our third overnight stop and here, two friends were enjoying a longer European experience. After an excellent evening meal with them, they directed us to the local camping ground. By then it was very late.

When we pulled up it was raining and windy. No problem. Like veterans we soon had the tent up in the dark, air-beds pumped up and went to sleep dead tired. We slept like babies. Next morning we woke to find the tent very wet. We could still hear the rain, but there was no wind anymore.

Peering out, however, gave us the shock of our lives. Ours was the only wet tent and car. We had camped adjacent to a fountain and all night the breeze had blown the "rain" onto only one area - our tent. Everything else was dry. Acute embarrassment hardly describes how we felt. Our decampment and departure could not have been more rapid. After this experience, the rest of the grand tour was a little more cautious.

More Fascinating Reading
'Cuz You Know You Want To!

Aurelius, Marcus *Meditations (Mark Forstater)*, Hodder

Bacci, Ingrid *The Art of Effortless Living*, London, Bantam

Beauvoir, Simone De *The Second Sex*, Pan Books

Botton, Alain De *How Proust Can Change Your Life*, Picador, Pan Macmillan, 1998

Botton, Alain De *The Art of Travel*, Penguin Books Ltd, 2002

Botton, Alain De *The Consolations of Philosophy*, Penguin Books Ltd, 2001

Burke, Edmund *Complete Home Fitness*, Human Kinetics

Cerexhe, Peter *Before and After Retirement*, CHOICE Books, 2000

Clarke, Ron *Total Living*, Pavilion

Chopra, Deepak *Ageless Body, Timeless Mind*, Rider, Ebury Press, 2003

Curry, Lisa *Health and Fitness*, Angus and Robertson

Dowrick, Stephanie *Forgiveness and Other Acts of Love*, Penguin Books Australia Ltd, 2000

Dowrick, Stephanie *The Universal Heart*, Penguin Books Australia Ltd, 2003

Edelman, Sarah *Change your Thinking*, ABC Books

Goleman, Daniel *Emotional Intelligence"* Bloomsbury Publishing Plc

Goleman, Daniel *Vital Lies, Simple Truths*, Bloomsbury Publishing Plc

Green, Bob *Keep the Connection: Choices for a Better and Healthier Life*, Hyperion Books, 2001

Longhurst, Mike *The Beginners Guide to Retirement*, Hodder Headline Australia, 2000

Lynch, Rob & Veal, AJ *Australian Leisure*, Longman

Macrone, Michael *A Little Knowledge*, Pavilion Books Limited

O'Connor, Bob & Wells, Christine *Health and Fitness over 50*, Crowood Press

Peck, Michael Scott *The Road Less Travelled*, Rider, Ebury Press, 2003

Powell, John *Fully Human, Fully Alive: A New Life Through a New Vision*, Argus Communications, 1989

Tacey, David *The Spiritual Revolution*, Harper Collins

About The Author

When I retired in 1988 I knew that I would have to remake myself and begin a totally new life. For forty years I had worked hard to achieve a successful career in Engineering, university administration, higher education and continuing education for engineers in industry. And it was satisfying. My career had been very focused. Electrical trade, associate diploma and three degrees in electrical engineering, ES Cornwell Memorial Scholar, foundation Dean of Engineering at what is now the Central Queensland University, with CQU naming the Frank Schroder Engineering Lecture Theatre. This was all heady stuff that meant I had had a 'full on', satisfying career for all those years.

Now, on retirement, the bottom had fallen out of all that, with no phones ringing for me to solve urgent problems. No plane trips to interview potential staff in foreign lands. No exciting new curriculum to plan. No meetings. So, what next?

In a nutshell I had no time to hanker after a past satisfying career. Instead of looking back I looked forward, trying to make every day a full and happy one. The short-term solution was easy - a four month tour of Europe by campervan from England to Turkey with my wife.

Retirees' Glee Club

Enjoying an afternoon of spontaneous music.

Music hath charms the savage soul to soothe

When we returned it struck me that no one had ever educated us on how to handle the biggest change that we will ever make in our lives. Forty years of concentrated work is no training for retirement. I knew I had to change and I did. I now had time to read what I wanted to read, including some philosophy in order to figure out where my life was heading. I then bought a button accordion and later a concertina and learnt to play both. This development has had an enormous influence on my life. For example, performing occasionally in Respite centres, playing folk music of yesteryear that old people loved was very rewarding. I took to reading and reciting Bush Poetry, and then even writing some! I increased my physical activity by walking, playing golf, badminton, kayaking and fishing. A small caravan took us on trips to far away places. These activities helped enlarge our circle of friends enormously.

I am the first to admit that right throughout my life I've been lucky, whatever that may mean, but retirement has provided me with the happiest years of my life.

Frank Schroder reciting poetry at the National Folk Festival Canberra 2002

New Releases from Central Queensland University Press & Old Silvertail's Outback Books

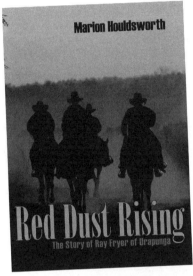

Red Dust Rising
- Marion Houldsworth

$ 25.95

This is the inspiring story of a northern cattleman who built up the Urapunga cattle station from nothing. From the 1950s to the 1990s, he lived rough and worked hard. He worked closely with the tribal Aborigines, made Urapunga a dry station, coped with the many crocodiles in the Roper River, fought against cattle diseases, hunted buffalo, built himself a homestead and survived.

The Charters Towers Goldfield Ashes
- Neal Sellars

$ 25.95

In 1949 on Australia Day weekend, 8 teams played 3 days of cricket in the searing heat in Charters Towers. They weren't to realise it at the time but, over 50 years later, Charters Towers is still hosting cricketers on the Australia Day weekend in the searing summer heat. The 8 teams have grown to over 170 teams, and is believed to be the world's biggest cricket carnival.

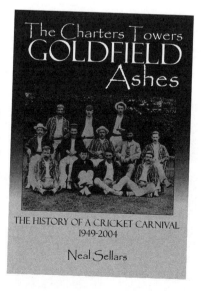

Showing Off: Queensland at World Exhibitions 1862-1988
- Judith McKay

$ 29.95

Many of us remember Brisbane's World Expo '88, but how many know of its ninteeth-century predecessor, the Queensland International Exhibition of 1897; or that between 1862 and 1988, Queensland took part in twenty-three world expositions?. This is the first ever account of Queensland as a global exhibitor, based on original research undertaken at home and abroad it is richly illustrated.

Best Stories Under the Sun
- Edited by Wilding & Myers

$ 25.95

Top Australian writers, winners of the Miles Franklin, Christina Stead, Steele Rudd, Australian-Vogel, Age Book of the Year and Commonwealth prizes, join with exciting new up-and-coming talent in this brilliant collection of 24 new stories, novel previews and retrospectives.

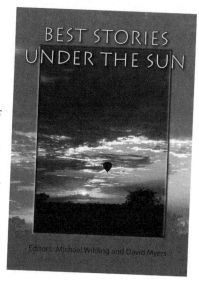

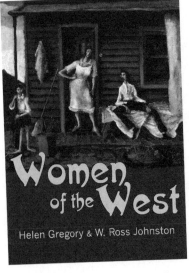

Women of the West
- Helen Gregory and W.R. Johnston

$ 25.95

This book tells the moving stories of over three hundred pioneering women of Queensland from the 1860s to the 1960s. It is based on the same research that produced the wonderful Women of the West exhibition at the Queensland Museum. If you're proud of being a Queenslander, this book is a must-read.

Cape York Peninsula
- Lennie Wallace

$ 25.95

This is a lively book, choc-a-bloc with hitherto unlauded heroes and heroines. Lennie tells of the feats of the early pastoral explorers, drovers and pioneers with special affection. But equally she tells us the stories of the sandalwood traders, the pearl divers and the gold and tin miners. It is history with hustle and bustle, heart and soul.

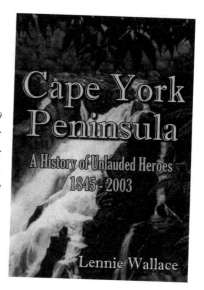

The Bush and the Never Never
- Gerald Walsh

$ 25.95

From Victoria River Downs to the Paroo, from the Darling to the Murray, this book evokes the eccentric characters, the swagmen, the pioneers and the great bush entrepreneurs who built pastoral empires. It also evokes harrowing tales of babes lost in the bush, historical treatments for snakebite, the myths of the bunyip and the visit by Archduke Ferdinand to the bush.

Portraits on Yellow Paper
- Roddy Meagher and Simon Fieldhouse

$ 25.95

28 short satiric texts by Justice Meagher accompanied by 30 black and white portraits by Simon Fieldhouse. The top achievers in law, academia, art & ecclesiastics in Sydney. Very funny.

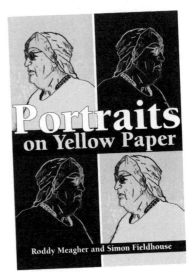

Other books by Central Queensland University Press & Old Silvertail's Outback Books

Half a Lifetime in the Australian Bush - Frank Brabazon Rudd $ 25.95

From Aramac to Yeppoon, from a commercial traveller, to a jackaroo, to manager of the Regional Development Bureau, it traces the first four decades of Frank's Queensland outback experience to the 1960s. Told with wit and good humour.

Jody's Journal - Marie Mahood $ 21.95

The exciting outback sequel to one of the few contemporary Australian bush novels for young children, The Nut Milk Chocolate Gang.

A Strong Song - Colin Macleod $ 25.95

The saga of the tragic confrontation of the Pintubi People with the white invaders of Central Australia in the period 1920s-1970s.

Patrol in the Dreamtime - Colin Macleod $ 25.95

A deeply moving book about the way Australia used to be. 19 narrators tell of their experiences growing up in the 1890s.

Horsebells and Hobblechains - Jeff Hill $ 25.95

28 northern cattlemen tell their stories. Features Lennie Hayes, Bruce Simpson, Roger Steele, Cec Watts, George Birch, Jack Travers and more.

Angels Don't go Droving - Jim Ditchfield $ 25.95

Dick Scobie is an outback legend in his own lifetime - childhood on the Birdsville Track, tough Territory drover, owner of Hidden Valley station and the only man in the world to run a cattle station from a wheelchair strapped to the back of a Toyota ute!

Diving Off the Ironing Board - Di McCauley $ 25.95

Di was a backbencher throughout those interesting Premier Joh times and subsequently Minister for Local Government & Planning in the last conservative government this state has seen for some time. A gloriously frank political memoir from a woman's point of view.

Barefoot Through the Bindies - Marion Houldsworth $ 25.95

A deeply moving book about the way Australia used to be. 19 narrators tell of their experiences growing up in the 1890s.

Horsemen of the Outback: Their Spurs and Their Spurmakers - Don J. Corcoran $ 25.95

A unique and irreplaceable book about the gifted horsemen who designed and wore many types of spurs in the Australian ouback. Richly illustrated.

Blood Stains the Wattle - Keith De Lacy $ 25.95

A love triangle set against the backdrop of the 1964 Mt. Isa miners' strike. An Australian working class novel.

Australian Cowboys, Roughriders and Rodeos - Jenny Hicks $ 25.95

A treasure trove of folklore, anecdotes and facts about the roughriding/rodeo culture of Australia.

Women Who Win - AnneMarie White $ 22.95

Stories of determination, heartache and joy from 10 of Australia's best known women. Includes Susie O'Neill, Kristy Hinze, Jacki MacDonald, Leneen Forde, Gina Jeffreys, Terri Irwin & Di Morrissey.

John Flynn: Of Flying Doctors and Frontier Faith - Ivan Rudolph $ 25.95

One of Australia's greatest outback folk heroes. Beautifully researched and written.

Flynn's Outback Angels - Vol's 1&2 - Ivan Rudolph $ 25.95

The pioneering women pilots and dedicated nurses that helped Flynn's dream of a mantle of safety come true. Vol 1 - 1901 - WWII, Vol 2 - WWII - 2000.

The Cattle Dog's Revenge - Jack Drake $ 21.95

Bush ballads and yarns from the funniest bush poet in Australia. Over 90 poems and stories to split your sides laughin'! Winner of an Australian Bush Laureate Award in 2004!

Legends of the Outback - Marie Mahood $ 24.95

32 of Australia's adventurers, pioneers and eccentrics. Includes Nat Buchanan, Jandamarra, Jackie Howe, Christy Palmerston and many more.

Icing on the Damper - Marie Mahood $ 24.95

The life story of a family on a cattle station called Mongrel Downs in the Tanami Desert.

Keep the Branding Iron Hot - Bobbie Buchanan $ 25.95

The story of Pat Underwood, owner of Inverway station, and the legendary cattleman Tom Quilty.

In the Tracks of Old Bluey - Bobbie Buchanan $ 24.95

Nat was the first European to cross the Barkly Tablelands from east to west, and first to take a large herd of breeding cattle from Queensland to the top end of the Northern Territory.

The Kokoda Trail: A History - Stuart Hawthorne $ 30.95

A unique account of Papua New Guinea's explorers, developers and barefoot mailmen. Made famous by the heroic ANZACs and fuzzy-wuzzy angels of WWII.

Legends of the Red Heart - Shirley Brown $ 25.95

26 legendary characters of Central Australia. Includes Carl Strehlow, Daisy Bates, Albert Namatjira, Ida Standley, John Flynn, Eddie Connellan and more!

The Ragged Thirteen - Judy Robinson $ 22.95

The Ragged Thirteen were expert horsemen and cattle duffers. They are in the heartland of Australian legends about mateship, bushmanship and survival in the vast reaches of the outback..

The Battlers of Butchers Hill - Lennie Wallace $ 23.95

A history of the explorers, settlers, battlers and dreamers who helped develop the Lakeland region in 1874-2002.

Nomads of the Queensland Goldfields - Lennie Wallace $ 25.95

Features Dr. Jack Hamilton as pugilist, prospector, physician & politician in the 19th Century goldfields from Gympie to the Palmer.

Walk a Mile in My Shoes - Tom Collins $ 21.95

The real-life story of a boots'n'all pioneer who did it tough in the early days from Toowoomba to Rockhampton.

Mackay's Flying Fortress - Robert S. Cutler $ 21.95

The tragic tale of an American flying fortress ferrying American GIs from the battlefields of New Guinea to Mackay in 1943.

Sin, Sweat and Sorrow - Lorna McDonald $ 28.95

A history that brings it all to life. From Great Keppel Island to the outer Barcoo. From breaker Morant to King O'Malley. Cattle-duffers, goldfield miners and the birth of Qantas.

West of Matilda - Lorna McDonald $ 28.95

A vivid collection of the original documents, photos and memorabilia from the 1860s to the 1940s.

Mayhem & Murder in Pioneering Queensland - Tony Matthews $ 25.95

Real life stories of crime, violence, murder, court cases and hangings in pioneering Queensland. Truth is indeed stranger than fiction.

Blackguards & Scoundrels of Colonial Queensland - Tony Matthews $ 25.95

A sequel to Mayhem & Murder *that brings Queensland social history one hundred years ago to a fascinating new life.*

Shipwrecks and Seafarers' Scandals - Tony Matthews $ 25.95

From the coast of Queensland to the savage isles of the South Pacific in the 19th Century. Massacres, the horrific plight of the immigrants & the stern processes of the law.

True Blue Queenslanders - Tony Matthews $ 25.95

Life sketches and photos of 18 Queenslanders who changed the destiny of our state. A colourful collection of wonderful unsung heroes.

Gold, Graves and Gallows - Tony Matthews $ 25.95

Crimes, calamities, mysteries, disasters, robbers, pirates and mutiny on the goldfields of Australia.

Unsung Heroes of the Qld Wilderness - Glenville Pike $ 24.95

Pioneering life in bush Queensland. Includes horse & bullock teams in the 1870s, the Queensland telegraph in 1869, drought and depression in the far west & Cobb & Co. in the 1870s and 1880s.

Crocodile Safari Man - Keith Adams $ 25.95

Harpooning and killing 20 foot crocodiles and making a film about survival in the Australian outback lead him around the world showing his home movie. Adventures in the Gulf and Australian deserts.

To order any title from CQU Press & Old Silvertail's Outback Books simply contact us at:

P.O. Box 1615, Rockhampton Qld 4700 - Phone: 07 4923 2520
Fax: 07 4923 2525 - Customer Service: cqupress@cqu.edu.au
Visit us online! www.outbackbooks.com
ABN: 39 181 103 288

Don't forget to ask for our *free* 20pp full colour catalogue!

Payment can be made by Cheque/Money Order, Bankcard, Mastercard and Visa.
Please make all cheques payable to CQU Press

Central Queensland
UNIVERSITY
PRESS